ITE

D1323555

CONTENTS

1. Introduction

2. Leaving the comfort zone

3. Goals and what to do with them

4. The temptations of defeat

5. You Either Win or You Learn

6. The power of positive thinking

7. Where Does Motivation Come From?

8. How to use your mind for growth

9. How to mentally prepare for a competition

10.   How to transfer this mindset

11. Imprint

1. Introduction

In sports and fitness we are constantly looking for the edge that will make us run faster, jump higher, get stronger, lift heavier weights, cover greater distances and just all around perform better than anyone else. In life we are also looking for that edge in all areas like finance, career, opportunities, relationships and more however peak performance is not always about nutrition, preparation, strategy or physical prowess, often times people who had been the best in their field failed because of one very crucial element and that was their mind. It doesn't really matter if you're a professional athlete or if you just play basketball on the weekends the principles and tools contained in this book apply to you and not just to sports either but we will dive in to this later on, for now we need to understand that like many sports professionals have stated over the years, it's all 20% physical and 80% mental, the mental aspect of sports is just as important if not more so than the physical part is.

Now a days more and more professional trainers, sports teams and schools are starting to incorporate sports psychology as part of their programs because they understand that even if all the pieces are in place your mind will either make you or break you when competition comes around or even when you're placed under stress. From performing at a world competition to just going to the gym on a regular basis, jogging even when it's dark or cold, training towards a half marathon, beating competitors even when the odds are stacked against you, keeping up your nutrition regimen during the holidays and more...

These are just some examples of how a solid practice of motivation and a positive mindset will make you succeed on any level. But do not think that this is simply limited to just sports and fitness, like I stated earlier, the principles in this book will help you perform at your very best in sports and they will also help you to find amazing success in all areas of your life, whatever that may be.

With the principles contained in this short book you will find the way to not only achieve all of your fitness goals better and faster, they will also help you achieve massive levels of success in all areas of your life if you're willing to take action and apply them, so the first thing I'm going to ask of you is that you make a commitment right here with me. There is a reason why you picked up this book and the reason is you want to know how to use your mind in the right state in order to perform better physically, so I want you to commit right now to reading the entire book from start to finish and to apply the principles you find in it to achieve your fitness goals and also better your whole life in the process.

Because in reality knowledge is not power, knowledge is potential power the power comes when you actually decide to take action with what you know, but just knowing is not power, it's raw potential. Commit now to reading the whole thing and then taking the necessary steps to convert that raw potential into pure and unadulterated power you can use to influence every single area of your life, from your job, your body, your performance, your relationships, your career, your finances, absolutely everything.

But don't get me wrong…

I'm not claiming to have any sort of magical formula or hidden knowledge that no one has access to, the truth is that these concepts are not new, I'm not re-inventing the wheel with this knowledge but I am bringing back concepts that have worked for ages and applied them towards performing a the highest levels in all areas of your life when you need it to.

Also you must remember that this doesn't mean that this is

by any means a shortcut or a magical sneaky get buff sitting on the couch type of situation, because there are no shortcuts, there is no way around it, you need to put in the work and put in the hours if you expect to see results, I cannot stress this point enough.

Any person who offers you some sort of magic button to solve all of your problems with no work, no effort and no mental energy being expended whatsoever is either a fool or a charlatan, so don't be foolish enough to believe that there is such a thing, this is not one of those books, the solutions offered in this book may seem simple but they are not by any means easy. Only those willing to put in the work and face their fears will succeed with these methods, in sports and in life.

I truly hope you commit to finishing and applying what you read inside this book and I really hope you enjoy reading it as much as I enjoyed writing it for you because I must say I had a blast.

Thank you and I will see you at the ending…

Zac Jenkins

2.Leaving the comfort zone

In sports much like in life there are many fears that go through a competitor's head before or during competition like the fear of losing, fear of embarrassment, fear of not performing to the best of your abilities and we all face these kind of fears every single day even if you're not a professional athlete I'm sure you've felt these fears even outside of sports, but the real greatest athletes of all time found ways to dominate their minds, their emotions and therefore act in perfect harmony with their bodies in spite of the fear thy might have felt.
One of the greatest basketball players of all time remembered by millions of fans and winner of many championships and accolades was Larry Bird.

Players who played with or against Larry Bird said that he was the most confident to the point of arrogance player out on the court, Larry was not the most athletic player or the fastest but he had an unshakable work ethic that drove him to practice to the point of perfection, developing not only physical skills to beat his opponent but he also developed his confidence in himself and is his abilities. And it was this supreme confidence that allowed him to win night after night in dominating fashion and maintain a very high level of play that earned the attention and the respect of coaches and players alike.

It's been said by many players who played against him that he would trash talk more than anybody in the league, in fact he would often go towards the opposing bench and tell them the play he was going to run and that they couldn't do anything to stop him. The most amazing part is that indeed they had no answer for him even if the knew exactly where he was going to be and what he was going to do.

This was no fluke and it had nothing to do with superior

talent or skills that he was born with, Bird's ability in the Basketball court had nothing to do with luck or any kind of freak occurrence. Larry simply had a very different way of thinking than most players, enabling him to go beyond his fears and perform at a higher level than any other player of his time.

Whenever Larry stepped on the court he believed his own hype, he believed that nobody could stop him and then turned it into a self-fulfilling prophecy by being very vocal about it and then backing it up with plays. The more he scored the more he believed he was unstoppable and so did his opponents and like I said before, Larry was not the fastest player or the most athletic but once he stepped on the court unlike everyone else in the game he was pretty much fearless.

Building supreme confidence:

Many other athletes have used this mentality to overcome their fears and perform at a higher level every single time they competed, often some of the top athletes used alter egos like it's someone else taking over their body whenever they compete allowing them to do things they wouldn't normally do as themselves and perform at a higher level than ever before.

But what's the reason for all of this?

Well, the reason is to get rid of fear, get rid of doubt and stepping outside of your comfort zone which is where all the truly great things happen in life, outside of your bubble. Whenever things are comfortable and nice you are not operating at your highest potential, if you have competed in sports I'm sure you've experienced this in the past. You're in the middle of training or a competition and you feel like you can't go anymore, your muscles start to ache and your mind is telling you to stop but something amazing happens when you decide to keep going…

You discover that wasn't your limit, in fact you still had a lot more gas in the tank if you know what I'm saying. It's nature, our brains are wired to protect us from pain and therefore it tells you to stop way before you reach your actual limit in order to protect you from pain, however most people don't keep pushing and never get out of this zone of comfort where there is no pain or real fatigue never realizing how much they can actually do when they get past that threshold.

This comfort zone is also where fear comes from…

Getting rid of fear:

What is fear? Fear is nothing more than worrying about things that have not happened yet or maybe never will happen and the whole reason why we have fear is to protect us from potentially painful experiences, if you burn your hand in an open flame the fear of getting burned again will lead you to be more cautious in the future and prevent serious injuries, however fear can be very damaging if you let it run lose inside your brain and contaminate all that you've worked so hard to get.

You see, fear like any other emotion you feel produces very specific chemicals in your body which can be additive. Yes, you can be addicted to certain emotions, this is why you often see people who are always angry no matter what happens, people who are always sad, people who are always stressed out, people who are always happy, and more. Regardless of what happens in their lives or what kind of circumstances they have got going on, they always find a way to feel this way and in this same respect there are people who always find a way to feel afraid.

Many people smarter than myself have placed a little

acronym on fear that goes like this:

False
Evidence
Appearing
Real

And too much of this emotion can lead you to perform way under your true potential, so in order for you to unleash your true capabilities you need to get rid of your fear and it is true what they say about fear, the best way to get over your fears is by facing them head on.

Often times athletes practice worst case scenarios in their training in order to remove the fear and to react in a calm collected way when competition rolls around.

This example may seem very extreme to some of you but ancient samurai in feudal Japan had a constant mental practice where they envisioned themselves failing and dying in battle, they understood that every time they drew their sword they may not live to talk about it but it was their constant practice and the acceptance of this truth that allowed them to become such fearsome warriors, they no longer feared death, they understood that it was a possibility and accepted it as such but the fear of making a mistake did not limit them anymore, they were free to act and fight with no fear in their hearts.

Hopefully you're not involved in any kind of sport that has the same kind of stakes involved although some do, like professional auto or motorcycle racing but constantly practicing your worst case scenarios even in your mind will allow you to get rid of many of your fears and perform at a higher level. Often times when a race car driver has any sort of problem and starts to skid out of control the advice veteran drives always give is to never look at the wall, always look at where you want to go and that's where you will go, this advice prevents many accidents yet some still do happen but being afraid of these accidents would only serve to increase the amount of times they occur, the reason why they say you shouldn't look at the wall is because looking at the wall makes you more afraid and keeps you from doing the necessary maneuvers to save yourself while looking at the track helps you keep your mind focused on getting back safely on the track.

As you can see being courageous is something that people often misinterpret as an absence of fear, people think that those who are brave have no fear and never experience fear but nothing could be further from the truth. Being courageous is not about not being able to feel fear, it's really about acting in spite of the fear or using the fear as something else, re-using the fear as excitement in order to perform better and acting when it is needed.

How to Escape the Comfort Zone and Destroy Fear

At this point you may be thinking to yourself "Okay, I get that I need to get out of my comfort zone and face my fears but, just how do I go about doing that?" well not to worry as we are going to get into just that right now.

The Greek philosopher Aristotle said something along the lines of our repeated actions being what defines us as human beings, therefore the quest for excellence is not found in one single action or moment in time but in our continual habits. If you want to get out of your comfort zone and face your fears doing once is not enough, one and done is not the formula to become fearless.

You need to continually practice doing things you're uncomfortable with and pushing yourself outside of your comfort zone, this is why some of the most successful people in the world include these type of things in their daily routines in order to be in the practice of continually stepping outside of their comfort zones and facing their fears. From taking a shower with cold water every morning to purposefully placing themselves in awkward social situations in order to face their fear of feeling embarrassed or being laughed at.

Developing the practice of courage

Millionaire entrepreneur and best selling author Tim Ferriss stated in his best selling book "The 4 Hour Workweek" that he often practiced some games with himself in order to place himself in awkward situations just to that he could get rid of his social anxiety and fear.
He would go to a bar or a restaurant where there were a bunch of people by himself and then proceed to lay down on the floor for no reason at all, he would go up to women and ask them for their numbers even if he had no intention on dating them he just wanted to get over the fear of doing it, he also practiced engaging in eye contact with people even if it made them uncomfortable just to get over his fear of upsetting people.

In terms of sports it's obviously practicing these worst-case scenarios, this is why in American football they do what is called a 2 minute drill which consists in trying to score in under 2 minutes because the time is running out. Also in tack and field they practice getting back from a deficit and regaining the lead for example and in Brazilian Jiu Jitsu they also start fighting from a very bad position in order to reverse or escape.

However my own experience in martial arts has led to discover one more level to this practice that most ignore but is absolutely crucial in order to really get rid of fear and perform at a higher level when you need to:

Stress

Stress can be a great teacher and it is a great tool to see if your can actual perform under pressure. Practicing the worst case scenario in a friendly safe environment is ok and you should do this especially when starting out but after this feels comfortable you should always find a way to introduce stress into the mix because in order for you to actually perform the way you want to perform be it in sports or in life you must be able to perform under great amounts of stress, because life is stressful.
It's not the same to drain three pointers in practice with just your coaches and team mates to watch you than to do it on game day with all eyes on you and the fear of embarrassment looming over your head constantly as well as the fear of failure that in all truthfulness is just another form of fear of embarrassment, the real reason why we fear failure is because we fear what others will think or say of us.

So practice this worst case scenarios with some sort of stakes, sticking to the example of basketball in order to place some stress into practice and make it a little more real you could introduce this idea to your coach who I'm sure will love it:

Do a pickup game starting ten or fifteen points behind with five minutes on the clock and the loosing team will have to do pushups or any kind of exercise you hate doing in order to introduce real fear and stress into the friendly pickup game.

You can create all kinds of situations like this one to expose yourself to real stress in a controlled setting or you can just go the route of just doing it and diving head first into whatever scares you so that it no longer becomes an issue.

The difference between those who achieve amazing things and those who simply dream about it is not how talented or physically gifted they are but how they handle fear. Get into the habit of getting out of your comfort zone and facing your fears constantly and I assure you they will no longer scare you.

Summary:

1. Set up scenarios of things that scare you
2. Purposefully face those scenarios
3. Add real stress to the scenarios
4. Repeat the process until you no longer feel frear

3. Goals and what to do with them

Goals are not just a nice thing to write in your journal or on your bathroom mirror but they are in fact one of the most important things you need to figure out whenever you're trying to achieve anything significant in your life, for to the people who don't know where they are going any road will take them there. Knowing your goals and being very deliberate about what you are going to do with your time and with your life is the difference between a life of success and fulfillment and a life of regret and failure.

Your mind is a very powerful instrument that can find any means necessary to guide you towards your goals but if you're not specific about how you want to get there any road will take you there.
Think about this: If I put a gun to your head and tell you that you have to lose twenty pounds by tomorrow or you're dead, can you find a way to do it? You might think you can't but if we chop your arms off we might be able to get you there fairly quickly, would you agree?

It's a successful outcome but that's not the way you want to achieve this because it brings pain in other areas of your life so you need to be very specific about what you want in your life and also about the things you don't want.

Your short term goals

First we need to establish your short term goals and these can be more powerful than long term goals for the simple fact that they are more manageable and achievable than the long term ones. Don't get me wrong, long term goals are absolutely invaluable and you also need long term goals in order to have a successful and fulfilled life but short term goals are the way you get to these long term goals in the long run.

Legendary NBA coach Pat Riley once had an experience with his championship Los Angeles Lakers where the team got to the NBA finals, they gave it their all but fell short of wining the championship in the last game of the final series. Pat then told his players that in order to win the trophy next year they had to get improve 25% in every area of the game. When you tell that to someone who just gave absolutely everything they had (or at least everything they think they had) their mind shuts off and sure enough the players pushed back and said, "you're crazy, that can't be done!"

After a while Pat came back and apologized to his team, he knew they had given their soul out there and to ask for 25% more is insane, he told his team that he knew that they could not improve any more, they couldn't get any better and so the goal now is to just focus on doing the same thing they did last year and hope for a better outcome.

When you say something like this to a normal person it may come off as understanding and even nice but as you can probably relate when you say this to professional athletes who are at the top of their game they get triggered and sure enough they said "Saying that we can't improve at all is crazy, or course we can!" to this Pat quickly said: Ok, if you want, all I ask of you is to improve 1%, just 1% improvement in each area of the game, that's all I ask of you. Free throws, blocks, steals, shots made, all areas of the game, just improve 1%.

When they all heard this they found the goal of improving 1% way too easy and therefore most players improved more than the 1% their coach had asked of them and then they proceeded to dominate the league next year and take home the championship they so craved.

This is the power of short term achievable goals, that then turn into stepping stones for bigger goals.

When goals seem small and achievable, you are more prone to actually do more than and actually surpass this goal as for long term big goals they tend to look way to big in the moment therefore it may cause you shy away from them and paralyze in fear that you won't make it and you will fail. But in fact these small goals are the way to get to those huge goals and that's what we are going to talk about next.

Your long term goals

Long term goals help you keep your sights on where you want to go in life, if you don't have a destination you will end up nowhere, so understanding what your destination is has to be a crucial part of what you do every single day, these goals may change over time and there is nothing wrong with that but they need to be crystal clear, you need to be very clear about what it is that you want to have happen in your life and what you want to accomplish.

For people like the all time great boxer Muhammad Ali his highest goal was to become the greatest boxer of all time, not just the heavy weight champion or an Olympic gold medalist which he did, but in fact become the greatest boxer of all time and this goal would lead him to behave differently than any other boxer at the time and to push himself harder than any other boxer before him, placing a higher standard on himself.

Ali won a gold medal in the Olympic games, he became the heavyweight champion of the world and he kept going, they stripped him of his title because of his refusal to fight in the Vietnam War and then he came back to win the title again, after that he lost and won the title again making him earn the title he so craved of the greatest boxer of all time.

Most boxers quit after the gold medal, they train so hard to become champions and their goal was just to win the belt bit once they do they are unable to defend it because their fire is gone, they no longer have a goal to shoot for. But not Ali, he won that belt and kept fighting because his goal, the vision he had for his life and his career was bigger than the belt, he had to become the greatest boxer to ever live and he did it, to this day many experts believe him to be the greatest boxer to ever walk this earth.

People with a negative mindset tend to constantly focus on the past, in order to develop a positive mindset you need to focus your attention on the present and the future back and forth. When you're driving a car you can't drive forward while looking backwards, you will crash! You need to look forward and have a destination in mind, that's what long term goals will provide you, the destination the aim for which driving becomes a great experience.

But also on a very important note, you should always enjoy the ride, because that is what life is about. It's not about achieving, all though that is awesome, you should always enjoy the ride towards your goal, towards your destination.

How to you set and use goals?

Most successful people have their goals displayed all the time where they can see them and they constantly write them down every morning when they wake up and every night when they go to sleep. The purpose of this is to take daily actions that will lead you to these goals through small actions that compile into big results over time, in order for you to achieve big goals you need to start achieving smaller goals that will lead you piece by peace to the greatest results you could ever imagine yourself getting.

But first let's learn exactly how you can set these goals, setting your goals is not a science in the sense that there no set way to set goals, some might tell you their way of doing it but it's different for every person it's more of an art. Finding what pulls you and motivates you like I said is not a matter of following a strict set of rules but more of a feel process, your imagination is one of the best mental tools you have at your disposal and it is the best way to identify your goals.

Think of a goal, something that you could have or accomplish that would make you incredibly happy and even just thinking about it makes you giddy and excited like a child.

Putting your dreams into action

List them all, take a piece of paper and write down your long term goals and I want you to be bold and forget about what you think is possible or impossible, let go of your mental blockages and limitations, if it excites you write it down.
Take out a piece of paper and write don the following things:

Have:
Write down all the things you want to have and like I said don't be shy about it because you don't think something is possible or not, if you want a flaming new sports car write it down, if you want a huge mansion write it down, all the things, gadgets toys that you would love to own, write down here.

Do:
Now write down all the things you would love to do, meet your favorite celebrity, speak in front of a crowd of your peers, own your own business, get married, win a championship, you name it. All the things that you've often fantasized about that make you really excited you should write down here.

See:
Next we are going to write down all the things that you would like to see, the places you want to travel to, the sites you want to see, if you want to be able to see the aurora borealis or a bioluminescent bay this is where you are going to write all of that down.

Next step is to get very clear on the process of attaining these things and this is where we are going to turn daydreams into attainable goals and it only takes a few minutes…

Now next to every item on your lists you are going to add the actual price of that thing or that trip or whatever it is you want to accomplish if it requires no money just leave it blank and if you don't know the price look it up. Now let's project this into a year's time so we are going to add up all the numbers from our lists and don't get scared by the amounts it will all get better later I promise.
Now to your total number add your normal living expenses like food, shelter and leisure. Next we are going to divide this final number by twelve and that's the amount of money you need to make in order for you to get all of the things you want next year, if you're already making that much money well you're in luck but if you are not it's only a matter of figuring out ways in which you can increase your income to that number and the ways you can do it are limitless especially in this day and age where the Internet has created such a leveled playing field for everybody who wants to make some serious money.

What if my goals don't involve money?

Maybe your goals aren't necessarily money driven…

It's basically the same process, you begin with the end in mind and you work your way back from there to develop an

actual game plan on how you're going to get there. Let's say for example that you want to be a professional football player, well the first thing you need is to figure out where are the best pro football leagues in the world? As of the time I'm writing this book that would be Canada and the US favoring the ladder, so if you don't live in those countries first step should be to get yourself there, second step is figure out their selection process, figure out what they are looking for, what drills are they putting their prospects through and what requirements do they put on them – now you can figure all of this out as most football drafting combines are made public through TV and social media – and then make sure you meet those requirements.
Next step is even if you are not one of the lucky ones to get drafted by a pro team you can go and try out for them as they often have tryouts to find local talent that they might have missed and if you don't get it the first time you have a whole year to get better and try again.

Note also that the traveling, equipment and training requires money as well so if you're thinking that you don't need to think about that you do and you should be thinking about it so plan for it as well.

Now that you're crystal clear on your goals now it's time to reinforce them constantly; one of the best practices many successful people use is journaling, every morning when they wake up they write down their goals on a note pad or a piece of paper, I believe in writing down two lists that will include your long term goals and your short term goals keeping you on track and focused every day in order for you to develop the habit of taking action every single day to advance towards that goal and knocking those short term goals down one by one until you start knocking down those long term goals one by one and that my friend is how you achieve greatness, through constant diligent action.

Summary:

1. Find out what your goals are
2. Get very clear on what you want
3. Get very clear on how to get what you want
4. Set up smaller goals and milestones to get there
5. Take action every day to make it a reality

4. The temptations of defeat

Most people tend to quit at 40% of their potential, not just in sports but in life in general, I'm sure that if you've practiced any kind of sport for long enough you know that whenever your body and your mind starts to give you signals to stop because you can't keep going, you discover that when you keep going there is a whole new level beyond that you thought your limits were before.
Quitting is very easy and tempting at times, which is why most people practice it on a regular basis…

If we were to simplify human behavior to it's bare minimum and get to the core basics of why we do the things we do, you could say that everything we do as human beings is either to gain pleasure or to avoid pain and that's it.

A professional basketball player plays because he gains pleasure out of playing basketball and the idea of not playing is painful for him. On the other side of the spectrum an alcoholic drinks to either avoid dealing with the pain he feels in the real world or to gain the immediate pleasure of getting a buzz, losing his inhibitions and feeling more confident even though he may know it's bad for him it fulfills that need.

Because of this your mind will constantly direct you to things that provide you with pleasure fast even if it may bring you pain in the future, and it will also steer you away from painful situations even if you know they are going to bring you pleasure in the long run.

This is why so many times you feel the urge to not go train and just stay at home watching TV, this is why even when you're competing you may feel a strong urge to just quit or settle for a certain result, there was even a case of a very successful tennis player who's name I won't mention to protect her identity but she never seemed to be able to win any mayor tournaments. Se started out great, blowing past her competition but her beliefs held her back, and because of those beliefs she started to slag and ended up losing the whole match.

What was that belief that held her back? Se believed that competition needed to be fair and even though she had the capability to shut out the other competitors she didn't because she felt bad for them, allowing them to catch up and then when she wanted to win it was too late. The fear of feeling pain by causing others to feel pain kept her from wining even when it was all she ever thought about and dreamed of, it wasn't until she got rid of that belief that she started to win and from that point on she started to dominate every single event.

Don't fall prey to the temptations of immediate pleasure and short term pain, always have your sights on the long term pleasure in order for you to avid the temptations of failure…

How to avoid the temptations of defeat

Before we understand how to avoid these temptations we need to understand a little bit of how our mind works and how we can use its own language to program in new behaviors and beliefs that will support your new desired behavior.

Like we stated earlier our brain is program to protect us from pain and direct us towards pleasure and even though this can sometimes be a good thing, when it comes to the long term it is very unhealthy. As your subconscious brain cannot see the big picture and will only focus on what's causing you pain right now and what will give you pleasure right now even if it is not good for you and in the long run it will end up hurting you or in some extreme cases, actually killing you.

This pattern could actually kill you

This is the reason why drug addicts have a such a hard time leaving their drug habits behind, yes there is a chemical addiction factor involved but even the strongest addiction is no match for a determined mind, the real problem for these people is that their brain is constantly telling them that not doing drugs is painful so we need to get out of pain and by the way, do you know what would bring us pleasure? Some of those drugs… And it's not that your brain is evil and wants you dead it just remembers your preferences, if you are in the habit of constantly avoiding your responsibilities and just getting high then your brain remembers it and your subconscious will reinforce it as the immediate pleasure of that dopamine rush is way better than the pain of dealing with the real world.

I realize of course that everyone is not a drug addict but I am using this example to show an extreme case of what we all go through as human beings for you it may not be drugs, it may be blowing off work and watching YouTube videos or spending way too much time on social media, it may be not going to train to stay in bed watching movies and eating ice cream but the process is the same.

How do we get break this pattern?

So how do we override this mental program that tells us to blow off work and watch another cute kitten video on the Internet?

The first step is to develop the practice of placing your conscious mind in charge, and for those of you who are thinking that their conscious mind is always in charge, think again. Our brain goes through millions of individual impulses every single day but we consciously might think about forty of them at best. Your subconscious mind is constantly running the show and it's precisely the source of that little voice in your head telling you to watch another video, you can call in sick today, it's no big deal.

How do you place your conscious mind in charge of the whole operation?
A lot of experts use what is called a five second rule, which is basically giving your mind no way out, and no room to negotiate, like when you try to get up early in the morning for example.
We've all gone through the typical morning negotiation with out brain once the alarms goes off to hit the snooze button, to sleep just five more minutes, that you can call in sick and keep sleeping but if instead of hitting the snooze button you actually count to five and then get up you give your brain no choice and no chance to negotiate, the next time your alarm goes off and you start to feel those familiar feelings of wanting to just stay in bed try this out…

Count one, two, three, four, five and get up right away and if you get in the habit of doing this every time you feel like not doing something you know you should be doing you will get it done regardless and you will avoid giving in to those primal urges of going for the immediate pleasure even if it means long term pain.

Another great exercise is to practice mindfulness, many top athletes and peak performers are in the habit of doing some sort of mindfulness practice every day, for some it's yoga, for others it's breathing exercises and for others it's meditation, really just see what works for you and stick with that but one of the most notorious mind bending human beings alive is Wim Hoff, this man is the only person to have ever climbed mount Everest wearing nothing but shorts and sneakers and he didn't even get the sniffles, the man continually swims in frozen lakes wearing nothing but a bathing suit and he does it by using some of these same mindfulness techniques.

I personally have tried his methods and they are very energizing and they also help create that mind and body connection that is necessary to master your life. I can't get into the exact method here, you can see it for yourself in his website but the basis of his method is mindfulness, breathing and cold therapy.

In the morning he goes through a series of breathing exercises that fill his body with oxygen and also places him in a mindful state – meaning that his conscious mind is activated the whole time – and then he follows up with a cold shower.

Cold Therapy

Now I know that cold showers are not necessarily the most attractive thing in the world but they are great for a number of reasons, first for health reasons it helps to reduce inflammation and promote recovery and secondly it helps to also activate your conscious mind and let your brain know that you're running the show and what you say goes.

Best selling author and life coaching pioneer Tony Robbins starts his day by doing a mindfulness exercise which he calls "priming" setting the kinds of emotions he wants to feel throughout the day and then doing a cold plunge every morning by jumping into freezing water and in his words he hates doing it, he dreads it every single time, it never gets easier but he does it for the health benefits but more importantly he does it because he is training his mind to understand that when he says he is doing something that's final and there is no other way around it.

In this same way you must train your mind to respond only

to your conscious mind and to keep your sights on the long term pleasure even if it means short term pain.

Summary:

1. Identify the things that keep you from success
2. Practice things that may be uncomfortable
3. Practice the "5 second rule"
4. Become extremely disciplined

5. You Either Win or You Learn

Failure is an inevitable part of sports and of life in general, the real test of a person is not how often they can avoid failing but rather how they handle their failures in order to learn from them and keep going.

Often times both in sports and in life we place these unhealthy expectations of perfection upon ourselves that do more harm than actual good when it comes to making progress and exploiting our true potential as athletes and human beings, expecting not to make mistakes and never failing.

For years I've practiced the martial art of Brazilian Jiu Jitsu and back when I was a white belt I remember there was this very intense competition I signed up for where you would basically compete against people from all levels and in my fist match I fought against a brown belt (Which is one belt lower than a black belt).

Needless to say I lost the match and I was pretty down about myself because I expected perfection from myself, I wanted to win even against someone who had around seven year more experience than me when my teacher came to me and said: You did great! I just gave him a look like he had to be watching some other match because I knew for a fact that I was horrible.

He said to me something that I never forgot and I hope that you will carry this with you as well…

"You either win or you learn… The only way you actually lose is if you stop working at it and if you haven't learned anything."

This was the moment I discovered something amazing, failure does not exist, failure is actually an illusion and much like fear itself, fear of failure is nothing but a figment of our imaginations.

Some of the greatest athletes and successful people failed miserably before they got to where they were but the thing that turned them into huge successes was not that they didn't fail but that they never stopped trying.

Successful people fail big

Michael Jordan, one of the greatest if not the actual greatest basketball player to ever live was placed in the bench in his college days for being too selfish, if Michael would have stopped trying and failed, he wouldn't have learned to be a team player and he would have never set foot on the court again in his life, can you imagine?

Another great player to have everything against him was Steve Smith Sr. one of the best receivers to play the game of football but he almost didn't get a chance to play at that position because everyone underestimated him. They said he was too short to play as a receiver, they said he was only suited for special teams, and it only took one opportunity for him to prove himself for him to place himself as one of the best to ever play the position.

Can you imagine if he would have just stopped pushing? If he would have just taken the comments he got from others?

Failure never materializes unless you allow it to, failure never becomes real until you decide to fail. You didn't win Olympic gold? There is always the next one and you have four years to prepare, you don't buy that? You're too old? Tell that to Dotsie Bausch, the oldest person to become an Olympic gold medalist in the sport of cycling at the age of thirty nine who trained so hard and got so good her coaches were basically forced to take her as part of team USA at the 2012 London Olympic games where she and her team won the gold medal.

No matter what your goals are, you can't actually fail unless you learn nothing or give up. Learning from your mistakes and moving forward is one the building blocks of success in any area of your life including sports.

The thing that Dotise Bausch, Michael Jordan and Steve Smith Sr. have in common is that they always learned from their mistakes and continued to push forward never giving up and never allowing their failures to become real and define them.

How to turn your mistakes into wins

Like we just stated the failure never becomes a reality until you give up, if you don't give up you've never failed you have just made mistakes and mistakes are to be expected. We live in a society to expects way too much from everybody and so we expect perfection from ourselves, we constantly expect ourselves to not make mistakes, to never fall, and to never fail but the truth is that you are going to fall, you are going to make mistakes it is a part of life, it's completely natural and the more you accept that the more you will realize that there is no reason to be hard on yourself or freak out if you make a mistake, you must instead do as my coach told me that day, learn from this and keep going forward.

When someone says they want to become a musician and when they hear them play it's awful, most people would say that they have no talent that they should pursue something else and that they should give up music because they are just not cut out to be a musician but imagine if you were to treat a baby learning to talk the same way…

You hear the baby try to talk babbling and mixing up words and then you say to the baby; "you should give up talking, you have no talent for talking, you should try sign language because you're just not cut out for talking".

That's utterly ridiculous, isn't it? Yet as crazy at it may seem it's the same thing. Anything in this life can be learned, any skill you want to acquire you can do it and you should not be expected to be perfect at your first try for some that may be the case and that's great but they will face challenges later on do not be fooled. Every single person on planet earth will fall, make mistakes and fail at some point or another but the trick is to know the challenges are coming and learn to roll with the punches, learn from these experiences and grow because of them.

In any sport there are average progression rates that people go through as they start to get really good and then they stagnate or go through what is called a plateau where they just stay at the same level but if they keep training and keep going they break through and start getting better again but after a while you will encounter another plateau and so on and so forth.

The difference between average and great athletes is they ability to get through these plateaus by either working harder than anyone else or by anticipating it and gathering knowledge from every possible source and breaking through.

And sports are an amazing metaphor for life, as in sports much like in life it's the moments when things look darkest that you must learn to get back up and keep going no matter what life throws your way.

Learn from your mistakes, because you should always remember that:
In life you either win or you learn…

Summary:

1. Expect to make mistakes

2. Don't spend time grieving your losses
3. Know that there is always something to learn from mistakes
4. Learn from them and move on

6. The power of positive thinking

Positive thinking is something a lot of people associate with new age ideas that are not really based on sound objective thinking but rather on completely subjective spiritual assumptions, people tend to believe that the mind and the body are completely different entities that have nothing to do with one another and that because of this thinking positively will essentially have no baring on the kind of results they will get in their respective sport and in their life.

Nothing could be farther from the truth…

The mind and the body… Actually, the mind ad the whole world around you are interconnected in a way that you won't even believe, but when you observe and you allow yourself to pay attention to these things you quickly realize that it's true. In order for you to feel any certain way your whole body must be involved in the experience of this particular feeling.

Using your body

For example, if you feel sad you tend to breathe slower, you tend to move slower and with small gestures, you talk in a lower pitch and not as loud, among many things. When you feel happy, it's the total opposite, isn't it?
You breathe faster, you move faster and with bigger gestures, you speak faster and at a higher pitch you feel happy with your entire body and this is exactly why the way you think can influence your entire life and therefore how you think can determine your destiny.

This is in fact the power of positive thinking, and let me clear by saying that looking at your problems and pretending they aren't there is not positive thinking this is called being delusional. Positive thinking is the ability to see things as they really are and adapting to them in order to produce a positive outcome.

The story of the four minute mile

A clear example of this is the story of the four minute mile; before 1954 people believed it to be physically impossible to run a mile in under four minutes, in fact everybody knew that there was no possible way that any human being on the whole planet could ever be able to run one whole mile in under four minutes until a man by the name of Roger Bannister came along and proved that belief to be wrong by actually running a full mile in under four minutes and you might think to your self that's great for Roger but he was a great athlete, what about everybody else?

Well that's the interesting part, the physical challenge that nobody ever seemed to be able to conquer became possible once Roger Bannister did it, after he broke the record more and more athletes started breaking the four minute mile and approximately 1,303 people have broken the four minute mile since Roger Bannister first did it in 1954. In fact running a mile in four minutes is now part of the standard for high-level runners.

What changed?

Did people use to run slower in the old days? Did we evolve as a species to run faster in the last seventy years? Not likely… In fact people use to run just as fast back then but every year there are people who can run faster and faster and faster through better technique, strength and conditioning, mobility, flexibility pushing the limits farther and farther and now something that use to be next to impossible has become common amongst high level athletes.

What changed was not the capabilities of people and it

takes way more than seventy years for any species to evolve and develop new features like faster legs. What changed was people's belief about this challenge, once Roger Bannister did it, it didn't seam impossible any more and those who saw themselves in the same level as Roger trained with the goal of doing the same and once more people did it, it became possible for many other runners across the globe.

This is how we work as human beings, once we believe something can be done we move toward it and start taking action but if we believe it to be too hard, too complicated or impossible we shy away from it because we want to protect ourselves from getting our hopes up, we want to avoid the pain of humiliation or the pain of disappointment so we never move on anything.

If instead we believe it is possible, even if nobody has ever done it just like Roger we can find a way to do it, because like I said our potential as individuals is limitless and a positive mindset can be the key to unlocking that potential for you to do amazing things in all the areas of your life.

No negativity allowed!

Now, just as important as knowing what a positive mindset can do for you and how to get it is knowing what a negative mindset can do to your results and to your life and how to avoid that at all costs.

Just like positivity, negativity can be contagious so in order to remain positive you must constantly consume positive information and surround yourself with positive people while avoiding negativity like the black plague. I have a sign in my office and it's quite simple in big bold letters is says very clearly "No negativity allowed in here" the day I put it up my wife said "Is that for me?!" to which I replied, "It's for anyone who sets foot in here" it's a policy, negativity will not be tolerated here.

Why? Because just like positive thinking can lead you do amazing things like shatter records and do what was once considered impossible just like Roger, negativity can lead you to sabotage yourself and destroy everything you've worked for in an instant and the worst part about it is that most people's negative thoughts are not even their own thoughts, they got them from somewhere else.

The news saying that the country is going to hell in a hand basket, your parent or relatives saying that you shouldn't aim so high because you will set yourself up for disappointment, your partner or spouse telling you that you can't reach that goal and you should just give up, coaches or scouts telling you that you will never make it in the sport because you don't fit their profile, you're too fat, you're too slow, you're to short, you're too tall, you're too skinny, you don't jump high enough, you don't sprint fast enough or any of the things you have probably been hearing all of your life that are not even yours to begin with but you've allowed other to place upon yourself.

So right here right now, I want to place a stake in the ground and no longer tolerate anyone's negativity, take up the policy of "no negativity allowed" don't allow people to be negative towards you even if they are doing it out of love or concern, don't allow it.

How to Develop Positive Thinking

Like we covered before positive thinking is not only something along the lines of wishful thinking, it is the lens through which we see the entire world and now we must also realize the positive thinking is also a practice and it is a constant practice that you need to engage with constantly in order to see results just like exercise, on the other hand we also covered how negativity can be detrimental to your success and eliminating it from your life as much as possible is also very important and now we are going to learn the habits you can start to develop in order to build up this positive mindset that will permeate into every single area of your life.

Thinking positively requires you to intentionally direct your focus on two mayor things:
1. **The Present Moment**
2. **The Things That Are Within Your Control**

Most negative people and people who are constantly depressed are always thinking about the past and either how the past was so much better than the present moment or how their past was so horrible that they are completely miserable today. If you are one of these people think of your life as a car in a highway and tell me what would happen to this car if you were driving it wile looking only through the rear view mirror? You would crash!

Whatever has happened in your past needs to stay there and you can still learn from that past or draw knowledge or inspiration from your past, there is a reason why cars have rear view mirrors but you need to keep your eyes on the road ahead in order to get there in one piece. The present moment is when you can affect the changes you want in your life, nothing can come of the past or even the future. The most successful people in the world are those who focus on both the present and the future by having a future vision or a destination and using the present moment to get there.

Also negative people tend to focus on everything that is out of their control, it become very easy to become depressed when you start to focus on all the bad things around you that you cannot control, however this will lead you to nothing other tan depression. If you tend to focus on the things you can't control realize now that even though you may not be able to control things like the weather, the traffic, accidents, illnesses, death, politics and more. You do have the ability to control the way you react to these things and ultimately how they make you feel and what you draw from them.

Focusing on the things you cannot control is like driving the car with you hands on you lap expecting other cars and things to get out of your way, if you do this you will also crash. Focusing instead on what you can control is like placing your hands on the wheel and steering the car to where you want it to go while avoiding other cars.

Make it real and gain control

So in order to develop a positive mindset you must continually focus on both the present and the things that you can control and a great way to do this is through journaling...

Just like in Chapter 2, writing down your goals everyday is a way to draw out a destination towards the future but it is also a way to stay on track in the present with actions that draw you every day close to your ultimate goals.
This in turn helps you stay focused on the present and what you can control, also another great practice for the development of a positive mindset is journaling about what you're grateful for.
It is extremely hard to remain negative and bitter when you're filled with gratitude so this is why many successful people are in the habit of writing down everything they feel grateful for the second they wake up and get out of bed, take 5 minutes every morning to write down all of the things you can feel grateful for in your life if your really allowed yourself to be grateful.

Putting good stuff in makes good stuff come out

Something else that's very important for the development of a positive mindset is that you must consume good information that will support this positive mindset and in this day and age it is easier than ever to do this, listening to podcasts, watching YouTube videos, downloading audiobooks, e-books and more, you can constantly consume vital information that will lead you to develop your skills, your mind and your positivity.

In the same regard like I said avoiding negativity is also very important to the development of a positive mindset as negativity just like positivity is extremely contagious and misery loves company.
So in order to avoid this negative energy you need to eliminate all of the negative things you consume on a regular basis, for instance I no longer listen to, read or watch the news in any way and contrary to what people might think I'm always up to date with the latest news because if it's important you will find out anyway.
The news channels are in the business of getting attention, viewers, readers and listeners and the best way to do that is not through nice and positive messages like "the crime rates go down" because even if that's the case they might try to spin it by printing something like "Are you safe in your own home?" planting fear and doubt in your mind in order for you to pay attention to the news and keep consuming it to know more in order to know if you're actually safe or not.

My father never use to watch the news and any time someone tried to get him to watch it he would always say the same thing; "Why should I watch it? It's always bad news anyway…" and he was absolutely right in more than one way.

Avoid news, avoid drama, avoid drama TV, avoid other people's drama, avoid negative people and most importantly don't allow yourself to become negative.

By continually practicing these things you can create a solid positive mindset that will have an incredibly positive effect in all areas of your life, spiritually, mentally, emotionally, physically and financially.

Summary:

1. Focus on the present moment and what you can control
2. Don't spend time thinking about what you can't control
3. Consume positive information
4. Avoid all negativity

7. Where Does Motivation Come From?

We often tend to think about internal or external motivation, we tend say things to ourselves along the lines of "if my boss greets me with a smile, it's going to be a great day at work" but what happens if that day your boss is in a bad mood? Do you then lose all of your motivation? Some people do…

But the truly motivated people are those who understand that all motivation is internal motivation, don't get me wrong, it is possible to be motivated by external factors however the way you interpret those external factors is all about what's inside of your head to begin with…

For instance, if you believe that the whole world is against you, when someone is kind to you and offers you're an opportunity you will immediately assign a meaning to this experience according to your beliefs, so if the world is against you this might mean that this person is either trying to extract something from you, make you look bad in front of others or set you up for a fall.
At the same time if your belief is that there is goodness in all human beings you will assign a very different meaning to the same experience, you might interpret this kindness as just human nature, a great gesture from this person, this meaning that they really care about you, and more.

Therefore motivation is an inside job…

The things that might motivate you are different than what motivates me it is sort of an art, finding what motivates you personally but using it and habitually creating motivation for yourself is a practice that you should engage in every single day. Motivation is not something you just get once and you're good to go, it's something that you need to practice every single day in order to maintain that same level of motivation.

Every single day block out time to develop your motivation and consume information that will help you stay motivated.

How to stay motivated

The best way to motivate yourself and stay motivated is to continually do things that draw you closer towards your goals.

Progress equals happiness and so you don't have to win the Super bowl tomorrow in order to motivate yourself you just need to run half a second faster, jump half an inch higher or lift two pounds heavier. To motivate yourself the best thing you can do is to take action and not just any kind of action but actions that will lead you to show progress in any area of your life be it physical, emotional, spiritual or financial, when you're moving forward you're also feeling continually motivated to do more be more and give more.

Do what you love

Something else that's really important is to always so what you love and now a days we live in a world where you can find ways to make money doing just about anything you can think of, from skateboarding to trading in the stock market. Doing work that doesn't really make you feel fulfilled will always lower your motivation but be cautious I'm not saying that if you don't like your job you should quit now and start a food blog because you're not there yet and I don't want you to be irresponsible.

If for example you do want to start a food blog you should keep your day job and write on the side, work your butt off and get your blog noticed by enough people so that you can start making money off of it and then once it's producing a good amount of income you could say goodbye to your old job and work full time on your blog. The point is that there is always a way to make money from the things you love and you should do the things you love even if they don't pay today, play the long game and get there slowly but surely.

Another way to stay motivated is to stay healthy, exercise and proper nutrition are an integral part of living and even you would all day at a desk having a healthy body allows you to be more alert, more awake, feel better and overall be more motivated because when you're getting better at one area of your life it spills over to other areas as well.

Summary:

1. Motivation is a constant practice so do it daily
2. Do the things you love
3. Take care of yourself
4. Remember motivation comes from within not from others

8. How to use your mind for growth

Your mind is the most powerful tool at your disposal and as you may or may not know many famous coaches have said that sports are 80% mental, this is why you must practice rituals that will help you use this tool to improve your performance and you whole life.
Every single day you should devote fifteen minutes at the very least to some kind of mindfulness exercise, some people prefer meditation while others prefer visualization, the choice is yours but this is important in order to direct your mind toward the kind of emotions you want to experience throughout the day.

The most useful forms of meditation are mindfulness meditation, which consists in first, directing your focus by eliminating all distractions focusing on the here and now by listening to your breathing and focusing only on this, after that you will be able to see your life in a more objective way and see the things you need to do more clearly and making better decisions because you are suddenly removing all the distraction and emotional hang-ups that usually could cloud your judgment in any given situation. Here you're creating a safe space where you can devote yourself to you and exploring your life as a whole from a place of calm and gratitude.

I won't get too much into meditation techniques as there are many other books with great information out there you can find on the subject, besides meditation is only one of the many tools you can use to develop your mind in order to achieve more so I am recommending it to you as a set of tools but I won't dive into it completely in order to get to more tools and leave your with a wide range of skills for this.

The power of the mind!

Visualization is also a great practice that you can incorporate to your morning routine allowing you to use your subconscious mind to direct you towards your goals like a heat seeking missile. Many successful people have used visualization as a powerful tool in order to condition their subconscious mind to always be in attack mode searching for ways to take advantage of every opportunity to advance forward and also develop powerful experiences you can draw upon to create the right state for achieving these goals.

In fact visualization can also be used in sports as it was very famously used by many great athletes in the past, one of these great athletes was heavyweight boxing champion Muhammad Ali who famously used visualization as part of his daily routine and even as an important part of his training for a fight, Muhammad would visualize every single move his opponent could throw at him to a science allowing him to see every possible outcome before the actual fight took place. Many fighters to this day use this same technique and this led to some of his most famous predictions, as in the press conferences leading up to the fight he would predict a win for himself and he would describe how he would win and also in what round he would do it in with total precision. After the press conference was done and the men stepped into the ring sure enough, more often than not his prediction would be correct to the last detail and the way he did this was through visualizing every possible outcome in the ring and how to respond to everything his opponent could possible throw at him.
I also mentioned that this is a great way to direct you subconscious mind and the thing you need to keep in mind here is that your brain cannot tell the difference between a real experience and an imaginary one. I will repeat this again because it's very important you get it; **your brain**

cannot tell the difference between a real experience and an imaginary one.

Meaning that visualizing with full emotional investment the conquering of your goals, performing the way you want to and generating the kind of results and the kind of interactions you want to have in your day will be stored in your brain as if you just lived it, helping you see opportunities better and recognizing familiar feelings when you are before a great opportunity.

Using your mind to affect change

The best way to affect changes in your life is to own up to everything, former Navy SEAL director and overall the most intimidating man you will ever see Jocko Willink calls this "extreme ownership". It's basically owning up to everything in your life including the things that you don't like and even the things other people do to you. Owning up to everything allows you to affect change because the way you see things in your mind will either cause you to conform to throw your arms in the air and say that it's out of your control or to take immediate action to change your situation.

The idea is quite simple; everything that happens in your life and especially the things you don't like are entirely your fault. If you don't have a lot or enough money, it's your fault, if you are overweight and don't have the health or the body you want it's your fault, if you don't have the relationship you want, your guessed it... That's your fault.

Own up to the good and the bad

Most of us like to spread the blame for out misfortune to other people or circumstances because it makes us feel better, it makes us look good to others and it also gets us some sympathy from loved ones, we all love it when others tell us that "it's ok" and "it's not our fault", we love that attention and we love feeling like we don't need to do anything because it's out of our control but the problem with this is that if it's out of your control you can't change it until you own it.

If you got into business with someone and that person stole from you and left you in debt and with a crumbling business in the verge of failure, that's not their fault, it's your fault! If you make it their fault and expect them to come back and suddenly develop a conscience you might die of old age waiting for that to happen, if on the other hand you decide to own up to it and admit that you shouldn't have gotten into business with that person in the first place your mind starts to work in a different way, you immediately start to think of possible solutions, you immediately start to solve the problems that are keeping you back springing you into action and getting you out of that situation.

You can't change anything in your life unless you own up to it, get into the habit of owning up to everything in your life, the good and the bad. And by doing so you will be able to change anything from your athletic performance, getting back from injuries, making more money, having better relationships and much more.

Own up to everything because if it's yours only then can you change it…

Summary:

1. Own up to everything
2. See what you can do to change your situation
3. Use your imagination through visualization to achieve success
4. Constantly condition your mind to succeed
5. Take massive action

9. How to mentally prepare for a competition

One of the very first people recorded in history to use his mind in order to beat his opponents even before he moved a muscle was the Canadian born boxer George "Little Chocolate" Dixon. The first black man to become a world champion at any sport, the reason for his success also came from a training technique he is credited with inventing. A technique so fundamental to the sport of boxing that it is hard to imagine a time when it wasn't being used by trainers all over the world.

Shadow boxing, and what is shadow boxing? Basically it's boxing with yourself, playing in your mind all of the possible outcomes you might encounter during the fight, going through every possible scenario and how to respond to it.

This has a lot to do with visualization, when a football Quarterback sees defenders rush at him thousands of times he no longer fears getting hit, he is able to operate with calm and precision in spite of the imminent hit he might take as he throws the ball but he doesn't have to actually get hit thousands of times to have this calm demeanor while he plays, he can do so by using his imagination to visualize the pass rush come at him full speed every time he throws in practice that when he sees it in the actual game even though he really didn't get hit in practice the situation now feels completely familiar to him because he has seen it in his mind many times, and as you might remember the subconscious mind cannot tell the difference between an imaginary experience and a real one.

This is the same way George Dixon created an imaginary experience of fighting an opponent that was not there, enabling him to be mentally prepared to face any challenge that might present itself during the actual fight, and this technique was in fact so successful that now all boxing gyms and many combat sports use this technique as a staple to this very day.

This same technique can be applied to virtually any single sport you can find successfully and not only that, you will no longer have the fear and worry of the unknown in the back of your mind as you've seen it all before, the worst has already happened in your mind and you overcame that, so this is just another stepping stone in your road to greatness.

The dos and don'ts of mental preparation

Dos:

1. When you're preparing for a competition the most difficult part is to deal with the fears, the anxiety, the anticipation and the unknown so in order to avoid all of that you need to direct your mind elsewhere, many sports psychologist recommend not thinking about the competition at all until your actually moments from starting as continually thinking about it will only lead you to mentally start to sabotage yourself, so before a competition distract yourself with music, books, conversation and don't pay any mind to the actual competition until you're actually seconds away from starting. This way you will be able to perform at your best and not have any mental blockages during the competition.

2. Eat healthy meals and avoid junk food, avoid processed foods and eat lots of fruits and vegetables, this will lead your cardio to be better and perform at a higher level on game day.

3. Get a good night sleep before the competition and also during training as sleep is a vital part of recovery and being well rested allows your to perform better both mentally and

physically.

Don'ts:

1. Don't ever listen to people who will come up to you and praise you before the actual competition takes place, don't accept praise until after you are done for the day because this might place heavy weight on your shoulders from other people's expectations and the fear of letting them down or hurting your reputation might hurt your performance in the end.

2. Avoid people who are constantly coming up to you to see if you're ready, this might even be your coach who is in all fairness more nervous than you might be, to which you should say something among the lines of; "coach, I'm ready, I'm ok I just need to focus, please stop asking me if I'm ready because I'm as ready as I'm every going to be". Nervousness can be contagious so don't let others spread it around and catch with it.

3. Don't try to do last minute adjustments and certainly don't try to increase your strength or cardio that same day or even the day before. The time for preparation has passed and now it's time to show up so trust in your training and just relax until it's time, doing push ups in the parking lot is not going to make a difference in the slightest.

10. How to transfer this mindset from sports to daily life

Throughout the entire book there has been a recurring theme, and that theme has been that all of the concepts and techniques laid out here in this book can not only be applied to sports but in fact can be applied to every single aspect of your life.

Like I said before, sports are the ultimate metaphor for life as many of the same things that can help you mentally for sports can also help you in your everyday life and at the same time many of the lessons you learn from sports are life lessons that can apply to every single aspect of your life if you really allow yourself to see the connection between the two.

For example the concept of mentally rehearsing your performance like "shadow boxing" can be applied in the same way to a business meeting, a presentation or even an argument with a loved one.
Spots are a lot like life in the sense that challenges will come at you from all directions constantly and learning how to deal with those challenges and still perform to the best of your abilities is the ultimate goal that will lead you to success in business, in your career, in your relationships and obviously in sports.

Practicing motivation, a positive mindset, visualization, meditation, goal setting and learning from your mistakes are things that allow you to have better relationships with your partner or spouse, better relationships with your family and relatives, better business relationships, better business and career outcomes, better performance in sports and better overall health as well.

So I hope you've played close attention throughout this

book and I want to thank you for sticking to your commitment, the one you made with me at the beginning of this book of reading the entire thing from start to finish.

Now it's time you honor the other part of your commitment and actually apply the things you've learned here because knowledge is not actual power, it is only potential power and it only becomes power until you actually take action and use the things you know, however most people don't do what they know.
Be different than the rest, dare to go where others refuse to go and work harder than anyone is wiling to work to get what you want. I know that you have it in you and I know you're that kind of person and you might be thinking I'm just saying this to sound cheesy but in all truthfulness I'm being dead serious, I know for a fact you are the kind of person who will follow through on this and the reason I know this for a fact is that you are reading this right now...

Every other pretender stopped reading on chapter one or didn't even open the book, you are here at the final chapter reading the words on this page as you kept your commitment to finishing it and now committing to apply what you've learned in your athletics and in your life.

Don't let the words on these pages stay as just ink on a page or dots on a screen, actually go and apply what you've learned here and convert this potential into actual power you can use to effectively generate the changes you want in all areas of your life, giving you the edge you want in your life, the edge to perform better in all areas and all stages of your life.

I truly hope you've gotten a lot out of this book and I want you to take action on everything you've learned here and apply it to your every day life, not just your sports practice but your entire life and share with me your success stories, I will be happy to receive them.

It's up to you now, as they say the ball is in your court and it's time for you to go out there and actually do the things that are necessary for making things happen in your life, as you now are equipped withe the tools to do so.

Go out there and make it happen.

Thank you for reading.

Zac Jenkins

Impressum / Imprint

Verleger und Rechteinhaber / publisher and copyright owner

gerodesign
Gero Gröschel
Wilhelmstraße 11
70182 Stuttgart
Deutschland/ Germany
hello@gerodesign.de

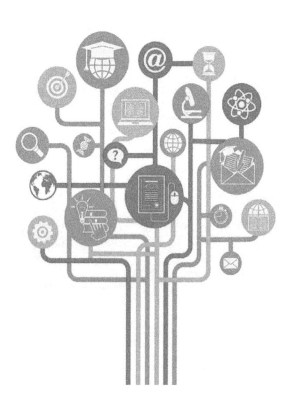